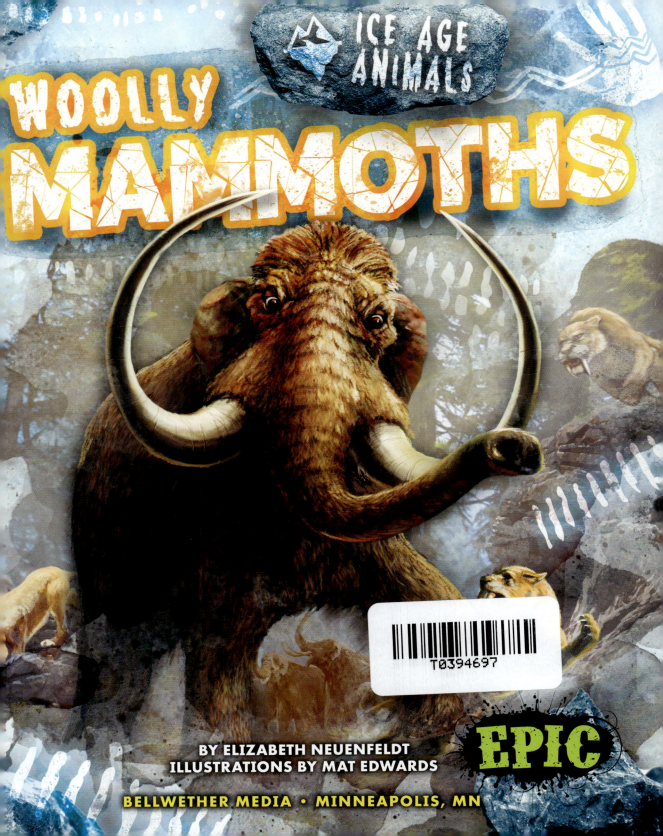

EPIC BOOKS are no ordinary books. They burst with intense action, high-speed heroics, and shadows of the unknown. Are you ready for an Epic adventure?

This edition first published in 2025 by Bellwether Media, Inc.

No part of this publication may be reproduced in whole or in part without written permission of the publisher. For information regarding permission, write to Bellwether Media, Inc., Attention: Permissions Department, 6012 Blue Circle Drive, Minnetonka, MN 55343.

Library of Congress Cataloging-in-Publication Data

Names: Neuenfeldt, Elizabeth, author. | Edwards, Mat, 1966- illustrator.
Title: Woolly mammoths / by Elizabeth Neuenfeldt ; [illustrated by Mat Edwards].
Description: Minneapolis, MN : Bellwether Media, Inc., 2025. | Series: Ice Age animals | Includes bibliographical references and index. | Audience: Ages 7-12 | Audience: Grades 2-3 | Summary: "Engaging images accompany information about woolly mammoths. The combination of high-interest subject matter and light text is intended for students in grades 2 through 7"-- Provided by publisher.
Identifiers: LCCN 2024019773 (print) | LCCN 2024019774 (ebook) | ISBN 9798893040449 (library binding) | ISBN 9798893041637 (paperback) | ISBN 9781644879849 (ebook)
Subjects: LCSH: Woolly mammoth--Juvenile literature. | Extinct mammals--Juvenile literature.
Classification: LCC QE882.P8 N48 2025 (print) | LCC QE882.P8 (ebook) | DDC 569.67--dc23
LC record available at https://lccn.loc.gov/2024019773
LC ebook record available at https://lccn.loc.gov/2024019774

Text copyright © 2025 by Bellwether Media, Inc. EPIC and associated logos are trademarks and/or registered trademarks of Bellwether Media, Inc. Bellwether Media is a division of Chrysalis Education Group.

Editor: Betsy Rathburn   Designer: Jeffrey Kollock

Printed in the United States of America, North Mankato, MN.

TABLE OF CONTENTS

WHAT WERE WOOLLY MAMMOTHS?	4
THE LIVES OF WOOLLY MAMMOTHS	10
FOSSILS AND EXTINCTION	16
GET TO KNOW THE WOOLLY MAMMOTH	20
GLOSSARY	22
TO LEARN MORE	23
INDEX	24

WHAT WERE WOOLLY MAMMOTHS?

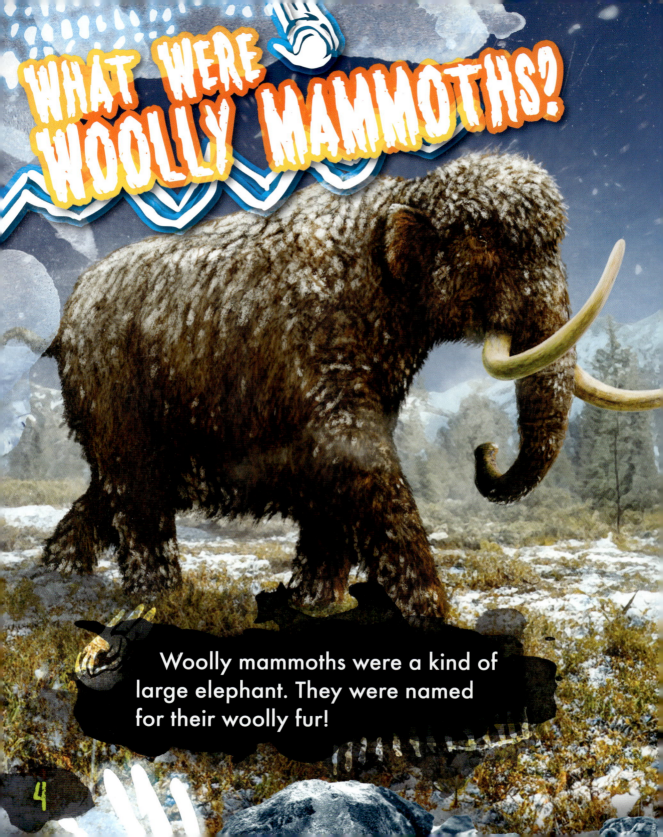

Woolly mammoths were a kind of large elephant. They were named for their woolly fur!

WOOLLY MAMMOTH RANGE MAP

● = range

EARTH

WHEN
First lived during the Pleistocene epoch

They first lived around 400,000 years ago. This was during the **Pleistocene epoch**.

Woolly mammoths had long outer fur. Their **undercoats** were thick. Their small ears kept them from losing body heat. They stayed warm on the cold **tundra**!

LONG LOCKS

A woolly mammoth's outer fur grew up to 3 feet (1 meter) long!

Woolly mammoths had **trunks**. They used their trunks to grab food.

trunk

Woolly mammoths were up to 13 feet (4 meters) tall at the shoulders. They weighed over 8 tons (7 metric tons).

Two **tusks** grew out from their faces. Some tusks reached 15 feet (4.6 meters) long!

THE LIVES OF WOOLLY MAMMOTHS

Woolly mammoths were **herbivores**. They ate grasses and **sedges**. They also ate flowering plants.

They dug in snow with their tusks. Then they used their trunks to grab and eat their meals.

WOOLLY MAMMOTH DIET

TYPE: herbivore

- grasses
- sedges
- flowering plants

11

Woolly mammoths were **mammals**. Females gave birth to live young. Young likely stayed with their moms for many years. Woolly mammoths may have lived in large groups. They traveled together.

young woolly mammoth

Young woolly mammoths faced danger from **predators**. Saber-toothed cats hunted them. Early humans also hunted them.

BUILDING WITH BONES
Early humans used mammoth bones and tusks. They made tools and homes with them.

predators

14

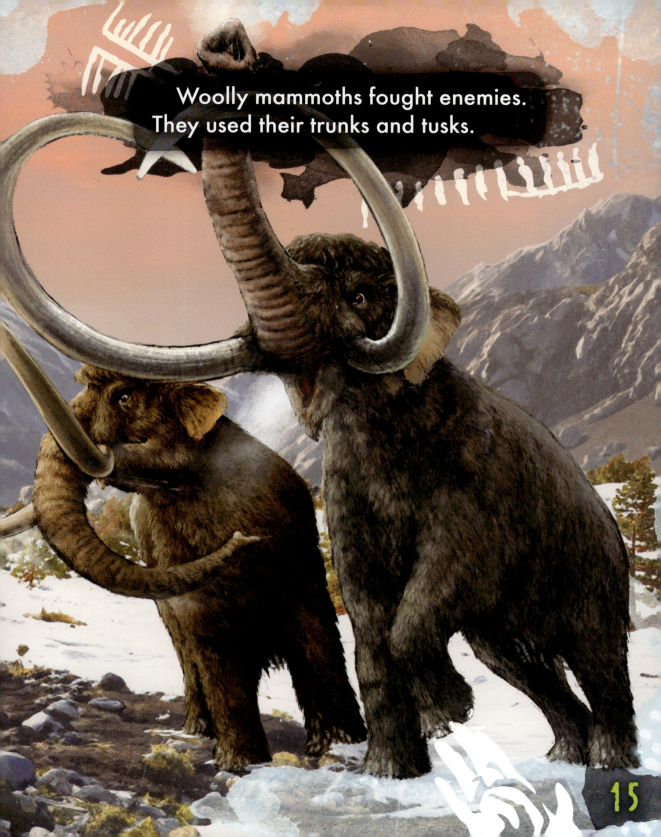

Woolly mammoths fought enemies. They used their trunks and tusks.

FOSSILS AND EXTINCTION

Woolly mammoths went **extinct** around 4,000 years ago. Their food likely disappeared. Humans may have overhunted them.

PRESERVED WOOLLY MAMMOTH

RUSSIA

NICKNAME
Yuka

DATE FOUND
2010

WHERE
Yakutia region of Russia's Arctic coast

MAMMOTH MEATBALL

In 2023, scientists grew a meatball in a lab. It was grown using small parts of a mammoth! But no one has eaten it. No one knows if it is safe to eat.

Many **fossils** have been found. People have even found **preserved** mammoths!

17

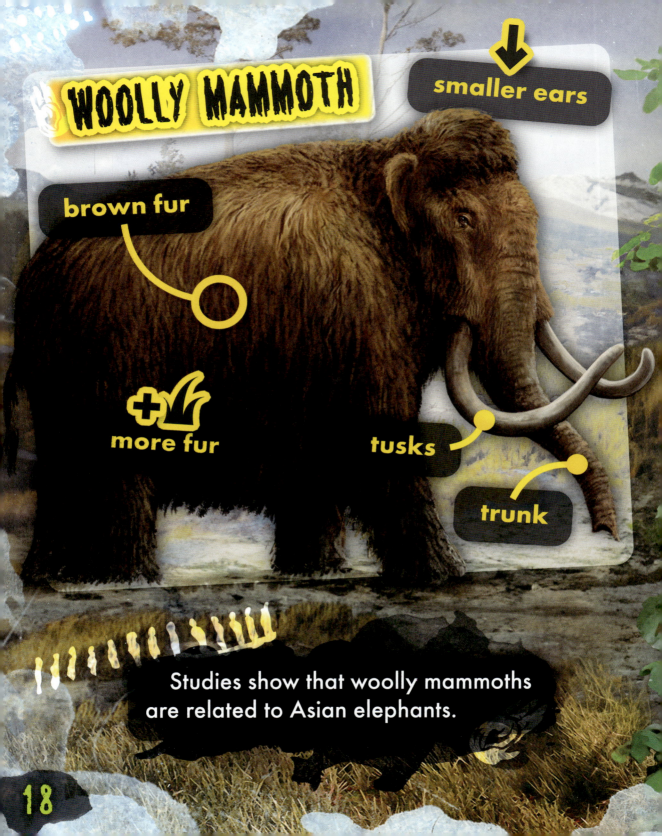

ASIAN ELEPHANT

- larger ears
- tusks
- gray skin
- trunk
- less fur

Both animals are known for long trunks and tusks. But Asian elephants have gray skin and almost no fur. They live well in warm homes!

GLOSSARY

extinct—no longer living

fossils—the remains of living things that lived long ago

herbivores—animals that only eat plants

mammals—warm-blooded animals that have backbones and feed their young milk

Pleistocene epoch—a time in history that lasted from around 2.58 million years ago to around 11,000 years ago and included the last ice age

predators—animals that hunt other animals for food

preserved—kept safe from being damaged or destroyed

sedges—grassy plants that grow in wet areas

trunks—the long, bendable noses of mammoths

tundra—the large, flat area in northern parts of the world where there are no trees and the ground is always frozen

tusks—long, curved teeth

undercoats—layers of short, soft hair or fur that keep some animals warm

TO LEARN MORE

AT THE LIBRARY

Gleisner, Jenna Lee. *If I Wandered With A Woolly Mammoth*. Minneapolis, Minn.: Jump!, 2023.

Murray, Julie. *Woolly Mammoth*. Minneapolis, Minn.: ABDO, 2024.

Neuenfeldt, Elizabeth. *Saber-toothed Cats*. Minneapolis, Minn.: Bellwether Media, 2025.

ON THE WEB

Factsurfer.com gives you a safe, fun way to find more information.

1. Go to www.factsurfer.com.
2. Enter "woolly mammoths" into the search box and click 🔍.
3. Select your book cover to see a list of related content.

INDEX

Asian elephants, 18, 19
diet, 11
ears, 6
extinct, 16
females, 12
food, 7, 10, 11, 16
fossils, 17
fur, 4, 6, 19
get to know, 20–21
groups, 12
herbivores, 10
humans, 14, 16
mammals, 12
meatball, 17
name, 4

Pleistocene epoch, 5
predators, 14
preserved wolly mammoth, 17
range map, 5
scientists, 17
size, 8, 9
traveled, 12
trunks, 7, 11, 15, 19
tundra, 6
tusks, 8, 9, 11, 14, 15, 19
undercoats, 6
young, 12, 14

The images in this book are reproduced through the courtesy of: Mat Edwards, front cover, pp. 4-5, 6-7, 8-9, 10-11, 12-13, 14-15, 16-17, 18-19, 20-21; Cyclonaut, p. 17 (preserved woolly mammoth).